GARDENING IN SLIPPERS

Gardening in Slippers

NEW POEMS FOR GARDEN LOVERS

SIR TIM SMIT
FOREWORD

LIZ COWLEY

GIBSON SQUARE

This edition published for the first time by Gibson Square

UK   Tel: +44 (0)20 7096 1100
US   Tel: +1 646 216 9813
EIRE Tel: +353 (0)1 657 1057

    info@gibsonsquare.com
    www.gibsonsquare.com

    ISBN 978-1-78334-075-0

Cover illustration by Dorrance.

Papers used by Gibson Square are natural, recyclable products made from wood grown in sustainable forests; inks used are vegetable based. Manufacturing conforms to ISO 14001, and is accredited to FSC and PEFC chain of custody schemes. Colour-printing is through a certified CarbonNeutral® company that offsets its CO2 emissions.

Printed and bound by CPI Group (UK) Ltd, Croydon, CR0 4YY

Foreword

Sir Tim Smit

Liz Cowley's writing is as if Pam Ayres and John Betjeman's poetry had had a love child. To say she is Britain's only humorous gardening poet is somewhat to miss the point. Liz is indeed both humorous and a poet, as well as a gardener, but you cannot write as side-splittingly, eye-wateringly, movingly well without a deep love for your subject.

For me, the pleasure of her writing is that its gentleness is not fey or wistful. It has the muscularity of someone who has something to say. Once the smile fades from your lips you are struck that behind what appears to be a light, self-deprecating lilt lies a passion signalling furiously that these words, if they are merely humour to you, mean you understand nothing!

It is a beautiful British art to be understated, and what Liz Cowley writes about is trivial things of a significant nature – the trivia that actually provide the glue to a life well lived. These lovely poems are about meaning and belonging, respect and affection, and they are tinged with wonder about and gratefulness for all life. Trivia like these are rare as hen's teeth. Give yourself a treat and embark on a journey that will cheer you up, and leave you feeling warm inside and thoughtful.

The Eden Project
Bodelva, St Austell
Cornwall

Still in Slippers

Outside at dawn again 11
The first celandine 12
What's lost to the frost? 12
Spring's out there painting 13
Plant talk 14
Moss makes me cross 15
Dear Primrose 15
Time to get the pond sorted 16
England's a pleasant country 17
Blackbird 18
These are a few of my favourite things 19
Fairy rings 20
March 21
Tulips 22
Hydrangea 23
Compassion 23
Just when I want to get planting 24
April 20th 25
Listening to a woodpecker 26
Mexican Orange Blossoms, aka Choisyas 27
Magnolia Grandiflora 27
A silent spring 28
Crow's nest 29
Our next door neighbours' Venus de Milo 30
The end of spring 30

Hello Blue Skies

You'll never dig alone 32
Hello blue skies 33
'I'm holier than thou' 34
Reading in the garden 35
The garden centre 36
Monet and Giverny 37
Will you, won't you? 37
In praise of slow 38
Grass seed 38
Underneath the arches 39
Hampton Court 39
Returning from Hampton Court 40

A salute to Edwin Budding   41
Lament for horse chestnuts   42
Periwinkles   43
Coming back from abroad   44
Grandma's footsteps   45
Website   46
Watching swallows   47
Chelsea Flower Show   48
The garden versus Wimbledon   49
My favourite Van Gogh   49
Disaster   50
'One can never have too large a party'   50
The primary colours   51
Going potty   52
Flower unarrangements   52
All too much   53
Why the rush?   53
'Gosh that is lovely'   54
Daisies, daisies   54
An open air concert   55
Can't   55
Lawns   56
11 p.m.   57
A favourite visitor in France   58
Oh, ground elder   59
Monkey puzzle   59
Ladybirds   60
Lunch in the garden   60
Evening mozzies   61
Useless creatures   61
Growing your own   62
Snapshot of a writer's paradise   63
Reading by a waterfall   64
Earthworms   64
What I wanted above all   65
The Eden Project   66
Sad   66
GM   67
Eleven a.m.   67

Mysteries   68
An oak can make you want to choke   69
Dear Fern   69
An English obsession   70
Do you grow cucumbers and mint?   71
Good Lord!   72
Why do I kill mint?   72
A 'can't be bothered day'   73
The Bambouseraie   74
Moving   75
Broke   76
Pelting down all week   77
One thing I don't like about my garden   78
Gifts for gardeners   79
Leaf shapes   80
Monty Don   81
Oh, for greener fingers!   81
July   82
Time to let things go a bit   83
Four-leafed clovers   83
The Marianne North Gallery at Kew Gardens   84
Plants and music   85
Why bees give me a buzz   86
Pubs   87
Weedy?   87
My first job   88
'Perfect happiness, even in memory,   88
Loss of freedom   89
Singing to cows   90
Blindingly obvious   91
Please keep your distance!   92
Salt-filled pails   93
Beatrix Potter   94
My smashing husband   95
War zone   96
However, gardening in a pair can work a treat   97
Why do we do all the weeding?   98
Gardening hands   98
Absentminded   99

Fred West   100
'Wind in the Willows' by Kenneth Grahame   101
A thought for Interflora   102
Roses are red   102
Tony Hannaford   103
Allotment wars   103
Sorry, garden   104

Woodland Wonders

Older gardeners   106
Younger gardeners   106
Where have spring and summer gone?   107
Autumn leaves   108
October   108
Remember, remember, the fifth of November   109
The fig   110
Solace   111
Built-in obsolescence   111
A lost childhood outside   112
Ugh!   114
Good tip for autumn   114
Out roasting chestnuts   115
Ouch!   116
In autumn years   117

Now is the Season of My Discontent

January   119
Wintering plants in France   120
December   121
A Jenny Wren   122
Annuals and perennials   123
Honesty (Lunaria)   123
Lichens   124
Adonis   125
When plants are dying   126
Too big a challenge   126
Christmas trees   127
The greatest present is one you can't wrap   127
December and January   128
An ever faster world   128

Still in Slippers

'Like me, you may slip out first thing
to have a look at everything –
a lovely time to be alone,
and see if anything has grown.'

Outside at dawn again

Best time to marvel at your flowers
before the busy coming hours –
the perfect time to be alone
without the stress or mobile phone.

The time to plan what you will do
with no one interrupting you.
A quiet time to come on down
and wander in your dressing gown.

A peaceful time to stroll out there
or take the nearest garden chair,
and think about your space a bit
and wonder what might add to it.

Just pottering around the lawn
can often make one feel reborn.
There's so much stress around today,
but out there it can float away.

And once you're through the garden door,
some things don't matter any more,
or far less than they did before.
I think that's what a garden's for.

The first celandine

The celandine, a heart of gold.
It's such a friendly little plant.
And walk right past a celandine
I'm sure you don't,
I'm sure you can't.
The celandine, the surest sign
that wintertime is at its end,
a gorgeous springtime visitor –
no wonder it's a gardener's friend.

What's lost to the frost?

What's lost to the frost?
What isn't growing?
Time to get going
digging and hoeing.
Time to start planning
what you'll be sowing.
Time for preparing
now spring is springing.
The weather is bringing
a whole new beginning.
Things are now budding,
plants are renewing.
Green tips are showing.
Lots to be doing!

Spring's out there painting

Spring's out there painting,
and busy she's been,
dipping her brushes
in more and more green.

Out there and painting
for hour after hour.
She's now using yellow
as daffodils flower.

Her canvas is gorgeous,
with touches of blue
as high up above her
the sun's peeping through.

Her palette keeps changing.
There's now lots of white.
Snowdrops have blossomed,
they've sprung overnight.

She's now done the cherry –
a cloud of pale pink.
A fabulous painting.
You stand back and blink.

A consummate artist
who captures the light,
and never stops painting
from morning 'til night.

Of all nature's artists
not one can compare
for lifting one's spirits
with colour out there.

Plant talk

Some flowers have a special art
of talking, reaching to your heart.
No words are needed, but they speak.
It's all part of their strange mystique.

I think I'd safely place a bet
you cannot pass a violet
without a pause, and some exchange.
No gardener would find that strange.

The very first spring daffodil
upon the kitchen window sill
will tell us that the winter's gone,
remind us that we're moving on,
as do snowdrops and the crocus –
beautiful communicators.

The cherry's merry, also vain –
it tells us 'Look at me again!'
Its blossoms always say 'Hello!
Please stay awhile, enjoy the show!'

Primroses have messages –
a chatty plant it always is,
and understandably quite vain
inviting us to look again.

Lots of plants are garrulous –
they speak and they reach out to us.
Listening, when we get the chance
is part of understanding plants
and part of what all gardening is.
So many plants have messages.

Moss makes me cross

Today I am cross
while scraping the moss.
No wonder I'm feeling so snappy.
There's so much to clear –
a load of it here.
A gardener can't always feel happy!

I'm cross with the moss
and now at a loss
while looking at loads more to do.
The time that I'm taking
to do all that raking –
my goodness, how fast it regrew!

This isn't much fun.
Four sack-loads are done.
And still there are more steps to clear.
I'm fed up with clearing,
moss keeps reappearing.
And finish the job? Nowhere near!

Dear Primrose

Dear Primrose, you so suit your name.
So prim, but pretty, all the same.
So sweet, so neat, a tidy plant.
Think of a better name? I can't.
The 'Prima Rosa' – that's nice too –
the name the Romans chose for you.
Dear Primrose, both names people chose,
so suit your primness and your rose.

Time to get the pond sorted

Time to drain out half the water
and get our garden ponds together
now that all the ice has thawed
and suddenly it's better weather.

Time to pull out blanket weed
(the plant that makes our ponds so green)
but leave in all the water snails
that help us keep the water clean.

Lots of thick green sludge to budge.
So heavy are the plastic sacks,
and lifting them – a daunting task
that's not too good for older backs.

At last the water's clear and clean.
That filthy task is done at last.
The sacks are out (and maybe backs)
exactly as in springtimes past.

Frogs and tadpoles, waterboatmen,
dragonflies and butterflies
and all our sleeping irises
will spring to life with bluer skies.

Not long to wait for water lilies
and kingcups golden as the sun.
It's worth the effort that it takes
to dredge our ponds, though not much fun!

England's a pleasant country

England's a pleasant country:
so lovely
in springtime
when new buds appear.

April's for showery weather
but still brings
me pleasure –
a time of good cheer.

Spring is a lovely season,
everything
budding,
a time I hold dear.

England's a lovely country
in springtime
while gardening –
and nowhere comes near.

And soon summer is coming
with sunshine
and colour.
I'm glad I live here!

Metre from 'yes is a pleasant country' by e e cummings.

Blackbird

I love your song, your golden tongue,
but not the cackle when you fly
each time another bird comes by.
It spoils the song that you have sung.

That squawking – grating to my ears,
so different from your lovely song.
It's raucous, and it sounds all wrong
each time another bird appears.

Your usual song is marvellous,
but not your shrieking of alarm.
Those other birds won't do you harm –
there's no need to make such a fuss!

I love your song – pure opera
with soothing bass notes, sweet and low.
But then, when you decide to go,
just what a cackling clown you are!

These are a few of my favourite things

Snowdrops and scillas and yellow primroses,
alpines, and violets tied up in posies,
flowering cherries, a robin that sings –
these are a few of my favourite things.

Clusters of daffodils, anything scented,
beautiful blossoms leave me contented,
gardening while hearing the flutter of wings –
these are a few of my favourite things.

Searching my garden for birds that are nesting,
planning my planting whenever I'm resting –
these are the pleasures that every spring brings –
these are a few of my favourite things.

When it's first light,
and things aren't right,
or I'm feeling sad,
I simply remember my favourite things,
and then I don't feel so bad.

From the metre of 'These are a few of my favourite things'.

Fairy rings

Year one:
A fairy ring – how beautiful!
A perfect circle on the grass.
Who put it there?
It's magical.
I marvel at it when I pass!

Year two:
That fairy ring – less pleasing now.
It irritates me when I pass.
It's mostly brown
instead of green.
I do not want it on my grass.

Year three:
It's not a fairy ring at all.
And now I find the ring a drag
with fungi, toadstools everywhere.
I'll have to smother it with slag.

My thanks to 'Gardeners' Question Time' for providing the solution.

'Well, basic slag applied at 6oz per sq yd will effect a cure but to prevent a recurrence, the turf should be hollow tined forked, then dressed with a mercurised turf fungicide or sulphate of iron solution (2¼%) or of potassium permanganate (1%).'

March

March already – time for sowing.
The days are passing, and too fast.
Time to try out something different
or stick with favourites from the past?

Ageratum or Alyssum?
Calendula? Begonia?
Callistephus? Centauria?
Gaillardia? Or Dahlia?
Convolvulus? Delphinium?
Or something new and trendier
like Aspera Hydrangea?

March already, best get going.
But what do you most want to grow?
Now, take a risk – or play it safe
with plants you've known since years ago?

Maybe better safe than sorry,
or should you be adventurous?
You're in two minds on what to grow
exactly like the rest of us.

Plants, in many ways like people.
Familiar souls are comforting.
Old friends or new? What should we do?
The same dilemma every Spring!

Tulips

Lovely when they're bold and upright,
but not when they begin to flop.
Some plants die out so gracefully.
Not tulips when their petals drop.

Death is part of life in gardens,
but when our tulips die, they sag,
always sloppy when they're floppy.
Mine soon end in a plastic bag.

The ones that flop soon get the chop.
I know that I should leave them be,
but hate them when their petals drop.
I wish they'd die more tidily.

Some plants expire so touchingly.
They seem to go with gentle grace.
But tulips don't, and that is why
I don't have many in my place.

Hydrangea

Too big for its pot.
I'm sorry for it.
It's struggling in there.
It's too tight a fit.
I can't get it out.
I can't get at it.
My fork won't go in,
more than a wee bit.
Hose the hydrangea
a good half an hour?
Still can't pull it out.
I don't have the power.
Roll the pot over?
Yes, that's what I'll do!
But, when I roll it –
it smashes in two!

Compassion

At times I'm sorry for our weeds –
unwanted species no-one needs.
I dig them up as gardeners do,
but on occasions, leave a few
while thinking (quite pathetically)
to dig them up is mean of me.
Great gardener I'll never be –
I'm lacking the brutality.

Just when I want to get planting

I plan a busy day alone –
not half of it upon the phone.
'Thought I'd ring and have a natter!'
(Girlfriend who adores to chatter).
'Just one more thing before I go!'
But is it only one thing? No!
'Guess what? I've joined the cricket club –
much nicer chaps than in the pub!
And one of them is such a hoot,
and in his whites he looks so cute!
I've found out he's a plumber too –
must get him round, there's loads to do!
The central heating's down again –
the bloody thing is *such* a pain.
Must let you go – I'm banging on.
Just one more thing, and then I'm gone!
Well, guess who I saw yesterday?
The chap I met on holiday,
you know, the one in Sicily
who fell a bit in love with me.
Oh, gosh – I'm banging on again,
I'm sorry to be such a pain.
Just *one* more thing before I go.'
It won't be *one* last thing – I know.
Just one? No, two or three or four,
and on occasions, even more.
At times, I stare at the receiver
and absolutely can't believe her.
'Just one more thing before I go!'
Why ever do I love her so?

April 20th

My goodness, it is almost May.
And what will you plant out today?
Well, maybe nothing. Time to sit
and think about your place a bit.
And this year, not rush into it!

Perhaps some kind of change is due?
Perhaps it's time for something new
or just another tub or two?
Now, what would most appeal to you
and what would you most like to do?

Perhaps a different colour scheme?
Contrasting colours? Ones that team?
Now, what would be your perfect dream?
Stronger statements? Bolder plants?
Time to plan, today's your chance!

It's almost May, the perfect day
to plan your plants, and keep away
from what is in the garden centre.
So easy is it when we enter
to fall in love with something wrong
as soon as summer comes along!

Listening to a woodpecker

The sound of its bill is just like a drill.
How can a woodpecker do it?
Just how can it peck without straining its neck,
and bore on hard bark and get through it?

No bird that I've heard, not one other bird
can beat it for boring and drilling
and making a hole, achieving that goal
with a sound and a speed that's quite thrilling.

What's more, it won't rest until a safe nest
is right in the heart of the tree.
It stays on its goal to make a neat hole –
fantastic to hear and to see.

Its speed is absurd, and no other bird
can do what a woodpecker does.
There's no other bird that I've ever heard
whose sound gives me quite the same buzz.

Mexican Orange Blossoms, aka Choisyas

Orange blossoms? Mine are white.
Whoever gave the plant its name?
Clearly someone needed glasses
or colour blindness was to blame.
The 'Choisya', that's so much better.
But Orange Blossom? That is mad.
I've never seen an orange blossom
on any Choisya I've had!

My good friend John Akeroyd (a Doctor of Botany) now tells me that Choisya is actually in the Orange family. But still, I think the title 'Mexican Orange Blossom' is a confusing name for a white blossoming plant.

Magnolia Grandiflora

Those leaves – dark green, with such a sheen.
Has someone been out polishing?
Those leaves – a dream. They seem to gleam.
That gloss is quite astonishing.
A fairy duster's been at work
to get them to that dazzling shine.
It's such a glossy, polished plant –
small wonder it's a friend of mine.
And as for all those shining blooms –
a fairy duster's been there too:
exactly like bone china cups
that someone's polished up for you.

A silent spring

Three nesting boxes,
but no birds in there.
No little fledglings,
and no nesting pair.

Gone are the blackbird,
the robin and wren.
Spring is too silent.
They won't come again.

Not when they're nesting.
Not in late spring.
Not in our cities
with babes on the wing.

Too many cats here –
far, far too many.
A streetful of cats
though I don't own any.

Dangerous for fledglings
when learning to fly.
Quieter my garden
each year that goes by.

Too silent out there,
too silent in spring.
Too silent am I –
one can't say a thing.

*I sometimes wish that there could be a law restricting city dwellers
from owning more than one cat. In the country, it's not so much of a
problem, but in cities it is noticeably quieter each springtime.*

Crow's nest

Our chestnut needs a hefty lop,
but with a crow's nest on the top
the pruning work has had to stop.

The crow is now protected.

They chopped down lots and lots of it,
but couldn't finish the last bit
in case the nest would take a hit.

It's not what we expected.

Today it looks most strange, our tree,
three quarters lopped, although we see
a crow who caws quite happily.

She cannot be ejected.

Our chestnut's now an oddity,
but there the bird still likes to be.
She's up there, quite contentedly,

though easily detected.

The tree may not look at its best,
but still, I'm glad they've left the nest,
now visible upon its crest.

How sad if they had wrecked it.

Our next door neighbours' Venus de Milo

They loved the Venus in their flower bed,
until the night the poor girl lost her head.
My neighbours saw a dazzling lightning flash,
accompanied by one almighty crash,
and then the next day, much to their alarm,
she had no head as well as neither arm –
beheaded by their eucalyptus tree
which crashed upon her unexpectedly.
Without a head or arms, a sorry sight.
Poor Venus had become a visual blight.
Of course, they knew exactly what to do.
With Superglue, she'd soon be good as new.
But then, while fixing her, a sudden clunk
soon destined poor old Venus to the junk.
Beyond repair, her body sliced in two.
How very sad, but what else could they do?
Sans arms, sans head, her torso sliced in half –
it's naughty of us, but we had to laugh.

The end of spring

Days are longer, plants are stronger.
Things are shooting, quickly rooting.
Lots of growth there, spots of colour.
You quite forget when it was duller.
Plants are spreading in your bedding.
You've even done the first dead-heading.
Summer's coming, grass fast growing.
And once again you're out there mowing!

Hello Blue Skies

'Hello summer!
Hello flowers!
Hello trees in summer bloom!
Hello flower shows and fêtes!
Hello flowers in every room!'

You'll never dig alone

A robin, feet away from you,
while waiting for a grub or mite,
alert to everything you do,
your slightest movement kept in sight.

He flutters off, he's had a scare,
but seconds later he is back.
You're once again a working pair,
and everything is back on track.

He's seen a grub, he's eating it
while keeping half an eye on you.
No fool is he, the opposite,
he knows he's clever, robins do.

You rest, he rests upon your spade
while singing you his gorgeous song.
A very pleasant friend you've made
by bringing all those meals along.

He sings, you do not say a word.
He does not like the human voice.
You know your silence is preferred.
You're quiet, you respect that choice.

You'll never, ever, dig alone.
You'll always have your robin there.
You'll never garden on your own.
There is, on earth, no closer pair.

Hello blue skies

Hello roses!
Hello lilies!
Hello colour everywhere!
Bye bye springtime!
Hello birdsong!
Hello time to eat out there!

Hello sweet peas!
Hello larkspurs!
Hello phlox and anthemis!
Hello fuchsias, hello cosmos
and clematis and irises!

Hello long days!
Hello sunshine!
Hello scents within the air!
Hello garden!
Hello blue skies –
the answer to a gardener's prayer!

'I'm holier than thou'

'I'm holier than thou' –
the hostas' anthem song.
And looking at my plants,
they haven't got it wrong.

'I'm holier than thou',
they sing to other plants.
A hosta with no holes?
There's very little chance.

'I'm holier than thou'.
My God, they truly are!
Compared with other plants,
they're holier by far.

'I'm holier than thou',
they cry out in despair.
A magnet for the snails,
a wretched sight out there.

'I'm holier than thou',
I always hear them cry,
and won't grow any more –
too full of holes, that's why.

Reading in the garden

Page 10:
I stop again.
I hose –
there hasn't been much rain.

Page 28:
and now I see
a most unhappy peony.
I tend to it,
it seems to be
in very urgent need of me.

Page 48:
I spot the gate.
It's peeling,
in a dreadful state.
An hour it takes
to brush the flakes.

Page 85:
I see a chive
that's struggling hard to stay alive.
I leave the book and take a look,
then water it, and quite a bit.

Page 92:
I pluck a weed
and once again I do not read.

Chapter 10:
I shut the book.
There's too much else
at which to look!

The garden centre

Here am I, in my favourite place
and with a smile upon my face.
The more I'm in, the more I pay,
and once again I'm here today!

Here am I, by the bedding plants.
And walk right past them? Not a chance!
Impossible – they're far too nice –
apart from the expensive price!

Here am I, standing at the till.
The girl is totting up the bill.
I've gone and bought a huge amount –
it's shrinking fast, my bank account!

Here am I, now at home once more,
my plants all through the garden door.
I'm looking forward to today,
despite the load I've had to pay.

Here am I, and out in the sun.
The plants are in, and every one.
But goodness, what I've had to pay.
I won't go back next Saturday....

Monet and Giverny

Never has a painter and a garden
been so very closely intertwined.
Never will a garden beat Giverny
if stunning waterlilies blow your mind.

A bridge that's Japanese, and weeping willows –
a garden that's more peaceful you won't find.
There is no other garden like Giverny –
a place to pause and marvel and unwind.

The perfect artist's garden is Giverny.
Enchanting planting – here, there, everywhere.
You've never seen Giverny? Worth the journey,
I'm absolutely sure you'll love it there!

Will you, won't you?

Will you, won't you, will you, won't you,
lay for lunch outdoors?
You take things out, you bring them in,
it's sunny, then it pours.
You take out chairs, you bring them back,
it takes you bloody hours.
Every time that you eat out
you still dread sudden showers.
In, out, in, out, changing everything about.
Will it rain, or will it not?
Now it's cold, and now it's hot.
In, out, and what a bore.
This is *not* what summer's for!

In praise of slow

A tortoise in the garden – today that's pretty rare.
As kids we always had one – a soothing presence there.

I've always loved the tortoise. The speed of things today
reminds me slow is lovely – far better in a way.

The tortoise never hurries, but seems to reach its goal.
It has a lot to teach us, this gentle, tranquil soul.

I'd love to have a tortoise – today life is too fast;
that soothing, calming creature I so loved in the past.

Grass seed

The next time that you're planting seed,
it's best to stay at home all day.
The ants will love it if you're out –
and quickly take your seed away.

The speed at which they steal our seed
is truly quite astonishing.
Ants – the last thing that you need.
They'll soon have pilfered everything.

Thousands will be rushing round
and colonies will soon be queuing
to get your grass seed underground.
Go out? *Last* thing to be doing!

The next time that you're planting seed,
stay home, and fetch a can of spray,
and check for ants from time to time.
And *never* spend all day away!

Underneath the arches

What is it about garden archways
that always make them so appealing?
Walking through a lovely archway
is always a most pleasant feeling.

Especially when a clematis
is climbing round in summer bloom.
There is no better, nicer entrance
to tempt friends to your garden room!

Hampton Court

At Hampton Court, there's row on row
of gorgeous roses at the show –
one reason that I always go,
though lots of names I do not know
or if they're difficult to grow.

But lugging them back home again
(or through the show) is such a pain
especially if it starts to rain,
so I don't buy.

How mean of me – I'll always go
and see those lovely blooms on show
but then think that it's best to get
one's roses on the Internet.
I say I'll get a better bet,
and walk on by.

Metre from 'In Flanders Fields' by Rupert Brooke (1872-1918).

Returning from Hampton Court
(A polite request from an anaphylactic)

Please don't bring back plants by train
and bring in bees and wasps again!

Please, please don't do that again,
for those who need an Epipen.

We hate to stab adrenaline
in public places that we're in.

We sit there rigid at your side,
and absolutely terrified!

We listen to things buzz about –
the bees and wasps just can't get out.

Exhausted, angry, on the wing,
they look around for whom to sting.

So do make sure at Hampton Court
that all the lovely things you've bought
are free from wasps before you board,
so passengers are reassured!

And thanks for reading this request.
I'm sure that you will do your best.

I find the show quite stupefying,
but getting back quite terrifying.

The show gives me a splendid buzz.
But wasps on trains? That never does!

A salute to Edwin Budding

Who on earth is Edwin Budding?
Have you ever heard his name?
He gave the world the motor mower
and surely merits greater fame.

While working in the textile trade
he studied fabric pile each day
shorn smooth by sharp rotating blades.
Could grass be shorn and cut that way?

It could! His clever motor mower
came out in 1831,
at last the end of shearing grass.
Now mowing it was quickly done.

No more scythes and no more sickles,
now mowing grass was superfast,
and tools soon started disappearing.
Their days were firmly in the past.

My warmest thanks to Edwin Budding –
a name all gardeners ought to know.
Here's hoping more folk think of you
next time the garden needs a mow.

Edwin Beard Budding (1796-1846).

Lament for horse chestnuts

How sad to see these lovely trees
are mostly smitten with disease.
A shame to see them spotted brown,
with leaves too early falling down.

The sight of them leaves me bereft.
How long before not one is left?
We have one here, and in our drive
that's struggling hard to stay alive.

It's huge, but not a pretty sight,
affected by some kind of blight.
A gorgeous tree it used to be.
The sight of it depresses me.

And yesterday, I sadly read
that all of them may soon be dead.
I know that ours may have to go
with all those ugly spots on show.

Too many trees are sick today
and evidently on their way.
And just what will our landscape be
without our splendid forestry?

Periwinkles

My periwinkles give me wrinkles.
Each year, a load of stems go black.
Each year, so many periwinkles
will end up in a plastic sack.

What's wrong with them? I've no idea.
I can't think what the illness is
and why it comes back every year
and makes the plants such miseries.

At Hampton Court they had a stand
to give the visitors advice.
'Oh good!' I thought, and hurried there,
though queuing two hours wasn't nice.

Long lines of people fidgeting
and lots of us were getting cross.
What's more, the woman next to me
was boring on about her moss.

But finally, my turn was there.
At last, I'd get some good advice.
And what's more, I would get it free.
The RHS don't charge a price.

I showed the chap a blackened stem.
He frowned, and then he shook his head.
'I'm sorry, love. You've beaten me.
I can't think why your plant is dead.'

My periwrinkles give me wrinkles,
and so does waiting in a queue,
especially when the RHS
don't have a clue on what to do!

Coming back from abroad

Two weeks away, and now you're flying
while wondering what plants are dying
or fading fast without you there,
starved of your loving, tender care.

Two weeks away, and it's been fun
to laze a fortnight in the sun,
but now you sit inside the plane
while fretting for your plants again.

You checked the forecast now and then
to see if there had been some rain.
There was at times, but mostly showers
and not enough for thirsty flowers.

You should have hired a handyman
and made a proper forward plan,
but then there was so much to pay
to go away on holiday.

And if you have a place abroad,
you never can feel reassured
the garden back at home will thrive
and everything will stay alive.

It can be so dispiriting
if no-one's been there watering.
Two gardens – one too much to do.
One garden's fine – but rarely two.

Grandma's footsteps

Grandma's footsteps on the lawn –
a sudden flash of memory.
It *can't* be thirty years ago!
It's not. It's more, incredibly!

Children playing in the garden,
our trees then only five foot high,
now reaching over sixty feet.
How time goes by! How it can fly!

Grandma's footsteps on the lawn.
'You didn't see me move!' 'I did!'
So much time has disappeared.
But still, I'm not dispirited.

The children – thirty, forty plus.
My goodness, time has flown so fast.
And now it's just the two of us.
How *can* so many years have passed?

Our gardens bring back memories.
No other places that I know
can bring them back as gardens do,
reminding us of years ago.

Voices, laughter in the past,
birthday parties through the years,
kids learning how to crawl and walk –
how quickly each year disappears!

Website

I sometimes throw small specks of leaf
at spiders' webs – beyond belief
how quickly spiders pounce on them.
I know I shouldn't give them grief.

Spiders, hungry, disappointed,
discovering that speck of green
is not an insect, not a fly.
I know I shouldn't be so mean.

But watching them quite fascinates me.
The speed they move – extraordinary.
How do they whizz across a web
and with such great agility?

And how do spiders spin their webs
so quickly and so beautifully,
and strong enough to live through storms?
A fascinating mystery.

It's said the strength of spider's thread
would even match the strength of steel
if made in ropes. Astonishing.
To me, that's why their webs appeal.

I've even seen a spider's thread
suspended in between two trees,
and watched the spider spinning it
quite perfectly, despite the breeze.

The spider started up one tree
and skillfully attached its thread,
then jumped on down in front of me
and to another tree it sped.

He climbed up in the second tree,
and once again attached the thread
then spun and hung a web from it.
Just seconds later he was fed.

I felt quite sorry for the fly,
but left the spider to its meal.
It surely needed a reward –
its energy was so unreal.

Miracles are on our doorstep.
They're never more than yards away,
there to see in every garden
and happening every single day.

Watching swallows

I look at the flight of the swallow
when feeding time's noisy and busy.
The flight path is so hard to follow,
enough to make anyone dizzy.

The swallows are swooping and diving,
so noisy, it's quite stupefying
when chasing and catching mosquitoes.
All of them call when they're flying.

I study the flight of a swallow,
but then I just have to stop trying.
The swallow is so hard to follow –
so agile, it's quite mind-defying.

Chelsea Flower Show

If you are like me
and may need to pee,
I don't think that Chelsea's your show.
You'll be stuck in a queue
(a massive one too)
and while you are dying to go.

If you are like me
and may need a pee,
I think it's a show to forego.
Instead of plant viewing
what you'll be doing
is dreading you may overflow.

What could be sadder
if your full bladder
stops you from seeing the flowers,
while you're stuck in a queue
of a dozen or two
and fearing your turn will take hours?

If you are like me
and may need a pee,
I don't think that Chelsea's for you.
What you'll be doing
is angrily queuing.
Please take it from me, that is true!

The garden versus Wimbledon

Whack! The sound of Wimbledon
floating out across our patch.
'LIZ, FOR GOD'S SAKE COME ON IN –
YOU'RE MISSING A FANTASTIC MATCH!'

'Thwack!' Centre Court at Wimbledon –
Federer and Andy Murray.
'COME INSIDE AND GARDEN LATER!'
I'm happy out there, in no hurry!

My favourite Van Gogh

A pot of chives – just one small pot.
Why *does* it please me such a lot?
A reproduction on my wall
that I can never pass at all
without a minute standing there,
or more if I have time to spare.
Some paintings simply change our lives –
and that one has, that pot of chives.
And now, when outside picking them,
selecting a nice healthy stem
or picking purple blossoms off,
I always think about Van Gogh.

Disaster

A Grecian goddess quickly bought
when strolling round at Hampton Court.
Disaster on our garden wall –
we didn't like our plaque at all.
On goddesses one can be keener
when they're ageing, turning greener.
The answer – yoghurt, brilliant stuff.
I cannot thank my friend enough
for telling us just what to do
to make our goddess look less new.
'Paint on a pot or two of it,
and that will age the girl a bit.'
Today, she is a gorgeous sight
a mixture of pale green and white.
These days she's a much-loved oldie –
so much better, looking mouldy.

'One can never have too large a party.'
Pride and Prejudice – Jane Austen

Oh yes, one *can* have much too large a party,
and even if the party's held outside.
Booze can get folk toppling over flowers.
Last time I had one here, I could have cried!

The primary colours

Create the world from seven colours,
including all the flowers and plants?
I would have said 'Impossible!'
I would have told God; 'Not a chance!'

It's hard believing all one sees
comes from a paint box quite so small.
It's one of life's great miracles.
Just seven colours for it all?

Red and orange, violet, yellow,
and indigo and green and blue.
Not many colours in the box
for all the plants God had to do.

Some gardens seem a mass of colours,
but all of them derive from seven.
At times it makes me just believe
there is a God, there is a Heaven.

As youngsters, we were taught the primary colours using the name of a mythical American, Roy G. Biv (Red, Orange, Yellow, Green, Blue, Indigo, Violet). I find it's still a great way to get kids to remember them.

Going potty

What a lot of pots I've got!
A blaze of colour when it's hot.
But tending them is often not
the fun it ought to be.

What a lot of snails I've got,
and picking them off every pot
is not a job I like a lot.
For me, it's misery!

What a lot of pots out there
and all need such a lot of care.
Those snails I simply cannot bear.
Anathema to me!

Too many potted plants I've got.
Perhaps I should throw out a lot.
So often all their leaves are shot.
Snails are at war with me!

Flower unarrangements

At times I plonk flowers in a vase
and get a rather nice surprise.
Unarranged, they can look better
and far more pleasing to my eyes.
Laziness at times works wonders.
Flower unarrangements can look great –
marvellous if I am busy
with other things upon my plate.

All too much

You thought you owned the garden,
but now the place owns you.
That's something you'd not noticed
until the workload grew.
You thought you owned the garden.
You did – some years ago.
It's telling you you're older.
Mine's telling me, I know!

Why the rush?

Why ever does a millipede
rush everywhere at breakneck speed?
Always in a fearful flurry,
never seen but in a hurry.
And all those legs! Why does it need
to go at speed, the millipede?
Afraid of predators, for sure –
that must be what they hurry for.
But what would eat a thing so wriggly
and multi-legged and also squiggly?
To swallow it must be so prickly,
and in the stomach very tickly.
Why ever would a creature need
to feed upon a millipede?
Uncomfortable those legs must feel.
It's surely the most awful meal.

'Gosh, that's lovely!'

As long as partners are encouragers,
it doesn't matter they're not gardeners too.
But gardening in a void must be depressing,
although I'm sure that many gardeners do.
'Gosh, that's lovely!' Oh, how nice to hear that!
A lonely hobby gardening can be.
Without reaction, far less satisfaction –
that kind of partner wouldn't be for me.

Daisies, daisies

Daisies, daisies, give me an answer do.
Should I mow you, or should I leave a few?
I rather like you growing,
so when I do the mowing,
I pause a bit, and think of it –
should I be leaving you?

Daisies, daisies, give me an answer do.
Should I mow you, or should I leave a few?
I rather like grass greener,
but should I be far keener
on daisies white – a pretty sight.
Should I be kind to you?

An open air concert

An opera of birdsong –
sopranos, contraltos, altos;
an orchestra of flowers in midsummer chorus –
bugles, trumpets, bells and flutes.
Sun in command, the world's hottest conductor.
And a free ticket
to the best seat in the house –
a deckchair!

Fantastic performers.
Glorious costumes.
Pure drama, and right on my doorstep.
I could sit here for ever.

Blooming marvellous!

Can't

There's no such word as 'can't'?
There can be with a plant.
Some plants I just can't grow.
And why? I do not know.
I know the soil is right.
I water every night.
They get sufficient light –
their spot is nice and bright.
I feed them as I should.
Their prospects should be good.
But still they die on me.
And why? A mystery!

Lawns

Some people, like my Dad, were born
obsessed with caring for a lawn
and tending it for hours and hours,
far less interested in flowers.

Some people wander round each day
while plucking weeds along the way,
and simply cannot ever pass
a dandelion in the grass.

And if the grass is getting high
or else in summer, getting dry
and suffering from bouts of drought,
they cannot wait to sort it out.

What people like that just can't do
is wait another day or two –
they simply cannot bear delay
They want perfection – and today.

Not me. I like a lawn that's green,
but overgrown mine's often been.
And mowing daily? What a bore!
I'll do it once a month, no more.

My patch does not make me a slave.
And if it simply won't behave,
I don't obsess like my old Dad
or let the weeding drive me mad.

I have a little London lawn,
which sometimes goes for months unshorn,
and what is more, a weed or daisy
never ever drives me crazy!

11 p.m.

It's raining, it's tipping,
my eaves are all dripping –
while here I lie dozing
and into sleep slipping.

It's raining, it's super,
it's far from heartwrenching.
It's spiffing, the garden
is getting a drenching!

It's raining, I'm dozing.
I don't find it boring.
It's lovely to hear it –
that heavy downpouring!

I'm sleepy, I'm dozy
as here I lie cosy.
My plants aren't complaining
not now that it's raining.

And I, too, am cheery
as hosing's so dreary.
And raining for hours
is good for my flowers.

It leaves me more free time.
It leaves me more 'me' time.
So, thunder – keep crashing.
The sound is quite smashing!

A favourite visitor in France

The deafening bee we hear and see
my husband calls 'A Messerschmitt –
twin engines and a crew of three'.
He's found the perfect name for it.

The Messerschmitt adores pink wine
and always climbs into a glass,
then sips away and can't climb out –
too drunk by now, the silly arse.

We always love to see that bee
and do not fear a mighty sting –
so drunk is he when he has sunk
he simply can't get on the wing.

We place a twig within the glass –
he flies off much the worse for wear,
just like a damaged Messerschmitt
with engines failing in the air.

We hear a noise of spluttering,
and half expect a trail of smoke,
but then his engines pick up revs.
He's off again, the lucky bloke!

A favourite visitor is he,
though no great pilot is that bee.
What's more he shouldn't drink and fly
and live his life so dangerously.

A truly splendid bee is he.
We really ought to know his name.
But Messerschmitt will do for now.
'A bar fly' is not quite the same.

Oh, ground elder

Oh, ground elder – how to get rid of you?
I've gone crazy over the likes of you!

You're all across my bedding
and many tears I'm shedding.
What can I do to uproot you?
Give me an answer, do!

Oh, ground elder, tried to get rid of you.
I've gone nutty, but you, you just regrew.

And still you're spreading, spreading,
and more of you I'm dreading.
What does it take for heaven's sake?
What can a gardener do?

Metre from 'Daisy, Daisy, give me an answer do'.

Monkey puzzle

The one thing I can't puzzle out
is why some people like this tree
with all its scales and monkey tails.
To me it is an oddity.

A tree I don't much want to see
and certainly don't want to touch,
and many times it's puzzled me
why anybody likes it much.

It's structural, I do agree,
but not a tree I want to see,
although I do enjoy its name.
I've found it fun since infancy.

Ladybirds

Teaching kids to count to four
is what a ladybird is for,
and sometimes up to six or eight,
though ladybirds I've seen of late
don't seem to have as many spots.
In childhood I remember lots.
I'm certain when I learned to count
they seemed to have a large amount.
I'm sure they helped me count to ten.
They must have had more spots back then.
Today they haven't got a lot,
or else my memory's gone to pot.

Lunch in the garden

Some people can sit out for hours
without the need to wander round
and have a look at plants and flowers –
that's something that I've often found.

Not all of us can gardeners be.
Some folk just want to chat and drink.
And just like you, I leave them be,
although it's somewhat sad, I think.

Some people just aren't curious.
A plant's a plant, and that is that.
I leave them be, they'll never see
quite where a gardener's head is at.

Evening mozzies

The whine of the mosquito
does not cause me alarm.
It's only when they're silent
they do us any harm.

That's when they are biting
and getting their next meal.
They cannot whine when sucking
and nothing do we feel.

But pow! One minute later
you know that they've been there.
You're itching while they're whining,
and bitten everywhere!

Useless creatures

I understand the maggot –
it does a clean-up chore.
But wasps and ants and woodlice?
Whatever are they for?

What's the point of maybugs?
And who needs centipedes?
And why create cockroaches
and creatures no-one needs?

I guess a million species
weren't made for you and me.
A gardener can be selfish
as I can often be.

Growing your own

Some give up growing vegetables
wishing they had never started.
Tending them is such hard work.
It's easy to become downhearted.

How nice to pick your peas and beans
and grow a row of lettuces.
But what an effort it can be.
Back-breaking it so often is.

If only growing vegetables
did not attract so many pests,
requiring months of vigilance
to keep out those unwanted guests.

Greenfly, blackfly, caterpillars,
and loads of maggots, that's for sure.
With all those pests upon the plot
I'm not sure what I'd grow veg for.

Digging, sowing, endless tending,
removing pests and fertilising.
No wonder it becomes too much
and giving up is not surprising.

There's nothing quite like 'grow your own'
or eating things from your own plot.
But plots like that take so much time,
and that's what people haven't got.

Snapshot of a writer's paradise

Grey shutters, and a lawn unmown,
a clematis that's overgrown.
Chairs rusting in the summer sun.
I'm sitting in my favourite one,
beneath an old crab apple tree,
its leaves and blossoms shading me.
Flowerpots, one left toppled over,
spilling clumps of purple clover.
Fragrances and butterflies,
above me, gorgeous cloudless skies.
A sixteenth century house in stone –
the perfect spot to be alone.
An ancient table where I write,
and sometimes to the fading light.
Tall hollyhocks, a gentle breeze,
no sounds, except for birds and bees.
Fuchsias, tall as the laburnums,
pink cyclamens among the rocks
and everywhere the fragrances
of lavenders and scented phlox.
Ivy spreading through the strawberries,
a rusty lantern on a ledge,
a wooden frog carved from a log
and herbs along each border edge.
A welcome here, each year for me,
good friends, and sheer tranquillity.
And hosts who kindly leave me be
while musing so contentedly.

Reading by a waterfall

Water falling, swallows calling,
frogs and tadpoles, dragonflies.
Ducks and ducklings,
sounds of birds' wings,
a heron – that's a nice surprise!
There he stands upon the rocks,
waiting patiently – so still.
A fish below! He's spotted it,
and now it's struggling in his bill.
I've bought a book, but reading it?
Impossible – too much to see.
I shut the book, the pond has won.
It's close to hypnotizing me.

Earthworms

Wonderful creatures! Splendid aerators –
you can't have enough on your plot.
Gardeners are lucky worms are so plucky,
improving our soil such a lot.

All worms are a treat – they burrow six feet
to aerate and strengthen our grass.
But why does a worm make some people squirm?
As gardeners, our worms are first class.

I know that they're wriggly and terribly squiggly,
but worms are a boon in our plot.
Worms are a pleasure, creatures to treasure.
And kill them? No, certainly not!

What I wanted above all

What children do not want to be
within their own house – up a tree?
And what a dream that was for me!
But not with the whole family.

Too many of us up a tree
would not have been a dream for me.
And seven simply couldn't be
within the same tree happily.

At six years old, and selfishly,
I wanted a tree house for *me* –
a place where only *I* would be,
a KEEP OUT sign nailed on the tree.

It would have been sheer misery
with seven of us up a tree.
The family would have fallen out.
(And out of the tree too, no doubt!)

*To have your own place and your own sanctuary up a tree is
probably one of the oldest childhood dreams – somewhere to read, to
hide, to dream – and look down on our parents! And it wasn't
always simply a childhood dream. Did you know that in Europe,
seats in trees (for adults) go back to Roman times, and that for
centuries in Italy whole trees were cleverly shaped and pruned to
become garden rooms?*

*The only tree house I ever sat in was the (very dangerous) one I had
at school – looking over the lacrosse pitch – a private sanctuary that
was never discovered, and constructed out of a few planks I found
in the school sheds. I am somewhat lucky to be alive and writing
this book.*

The Eden Project

A miracle of geometry
as much as natural history,
where wit of man and works of God
combine in perfect harmony.
Adjoining domes, the ideal homes
for plants from different territory –
as much a monument to man
as nature's ingenuity.
Vast mushrooms made of scores of cells –
those domes, or 'biomes' are to me,
as stunning as the plants they house
in awe-inspiring unity.

Sad

On days you wake in misery
(and maybe unaccountably)
a garden is the place to be.
At least, that always works for me.

Just stroll around a little bit.
If sad, you can float out of it.
A garden has great healing powers
as do many plants and flowers.

A place of calm and sanctuary.
The space to think, and silently –
that's excellent psychiatry.
So soothing is tranquillity.

On days you wake up in despair,
it's good to have a garden there,
and furthermore, it can be where
you find the kindest mental care.

GM

It can't be long before a rose that's blue –
true blue, and also blooms the whole year through.

And why should grass be green, not red or blue?
It's only what we're best accustomed to.

Of course our grass needs chlorophyll, that's true.
But change that, scientists will surely do.

Not one of us will live to get the chance
to see how they might look, our many plants.

Astonishing what hybridists can do.
It sometimes worries me. And does it you?

Eleven a.m.

Still in my dressing gown. Where is my pride?
And the door bell has rung. Ouch! Better hide!
It's lucky I have a number of trees.
Do please stop ringing, and go away please!
Out in my dressing gown, strolling about –
oh, so embarrassing when I'm caught out!

Mysteries

Ever seen a flower open?
Of course your answer will be 'No',
except, perhaps on television
and in a natural history show.

Plants do things behind our backs –
they do not welcome witnesses.
They far prefer their secret lives.
It's one of life's great mysteries.

Petals always close and open
without our ever noticing.
I often wonder why they're shy
and always hiding everything.

Only a stop motion programme
can take us to their hidden world,
showing us how flowers open
and how their blossoms are unfurled.

Plants are private, all have secrets
and ones they don't want us to know.
We'll never truly understand them –
one reason why I love them so.

An oak can make you want to choke

I warn you – do not have an oak
too near your house. You'll end up broke.
It grows so fast, needs constant lopping,
and once a year, quite heavy chopping
with bills that make you want to choke.

And all the leaves – beyond belief!
You'll find them a huge source of grief.
All year round its leaves are falling.
The mess oaks make is quite appalling –
you'll never get a day's relief.

Oaks can quite exhaust your patience
(and they're rotten for foundations)
so please take this advice from me –
it's not the wisest choice of tree
unless it's planted distantly –
not one of God's best creations!

Dear Fern

Dear Fern, you earn a place in gardens.
What's more, a place in gardeners' hearts.
You always make the grade in shade,
miraculous in sun-starved parts.
Such lovely whorls, then sweeping fronds
content to live without the sun.
What other shady character gives back as much?
There isn't one.

An English obsession

In England, most of us were born
to love (and need) a patch of lawn.
However did it come to pass –
our yearning for a patch of grass?

A croquet pitch, a bowling green –
that's also such an English scene.
And so too is a tennis court
of emerald green, the grass cut short.

I don't think that it will ever pass –
our very English love of grass
or else our strong and national pride
in having a nice lawn outside.

Our dream – to keep it perfect green
without a daisy on the scene,
and flat as is a billiard table
and mown each week if we are able.

We couldn't stand to be the owner
of lawns in spots like Arizona
or anywhere the sun is higher
and grass looks scorched by prairie fire.

More people here are simply born
to love a swathe of smooth green lawn.
And just how English that love is –
one of our eccentricities!

Do you grow cucumbers and mint?

I served this soup to Albert Roux.
A terrifying thing to do.
He didn't have one bowl, but *three*!
I wallowed in the flattery.
Whose recipe? I wish I knew.
And so, I'm sure, would Albert Roux.
I know acknowledgements are due,
but don't know who to give them to.

Chilled Cucumber and Mint Soup – Serves 6
2 cucumbers
1 bunch (about 12 stalks) mint
1 oz butter
1 small onion
¾ pint chicken stock
1 rounded tablespoon flour
½ pint milk
1 carton soured cream
salt and freshly-milled pepper

Cut about two inches off one of the cucumbers and set aside for the garnish. Peel both cucumbers cut in half lengthways, remove seeds and cut the flesh coarsely.

Melt the butter in a saucepan. Peel and chop the onion, add to the pan and sauté gently until the onion is soft but not brown. Add the cucumber and mint. Stir to mix, then add the chicken stock. Bring to the boil ad simmer for twenty minutes.

Blend the flour with the milk – stir or whisk, there should be no lumps. Add a little of the hot chicken stock from the pan, blend well and then stir into the soup. Bring to the boil, simmer for two to three minutes, then draw off the heat. Rub the soup through a sieve or purée in an electric blender. Allow to cool. Add the soured cream and then chill well.

Garnish with thin slices of preserved cucumber and serve.

Good Lord!

Sitting one day in the garden
(and brought right to my knees)
I asked my husband crossly
'Could *you* do something please?'
Good Lord! He fetched the mower!
They can surprise us, men.
And the sound when it was switched on
was the sound of a great Amen!
At times, a bit of help is nice –
it's most appreciated
especially if that help is rare
or else somewhat belated!

Why do I kill mint?

I've often killed my mint.
It doesn't like me much.
It's something in my skin.
It seems to hate my touch.

Now gloves I have to wear
before I touch the plant.
It hates the skin I'm in,
and live with it, it can't.

I pick my mint most days.
A herb I really love.
A herb that now likes me,
because I wear a glove.

A 'can't be bothered day'

Today's a 'can't be bothered' day.
This week's a 'can't be bothered' week.
I can't be bothered gardening,
and anyway, the weather's bleak.

At times all gardeners need a break,
and then it's such a nice surprise
the next time we stroll round again –
we see the place with different eyes.

It's then that inspiration comes,
together with a rush of pleasure.
We picture plants that could look great,
the best time to get plans together.

I always go outside at dawn,
but maybe not again that day,
and sometimes take a longer break
and put my garden tools away.

.

I like a 'can't be bothered' week.
I like a 'can't be bothered' day.
Gardens can be all the nicer
because you've spent some time away.

The Bambouseraie

Now, who would ever grow bamboo?
Amazes me that people do.

It's not a plant I'd ever choose.
However, I adore Anduze.

Anduze, in Languedoc, in France –
do visit if you get the chance.

One day, see the 'Bambouseraie'.
A lovely way to spend a day.

The bamboos tower into the sky –
I've never seen them grow so high.

Stroll down a gorgeous avenue
with massive branches shading you.

A truly splendid sight is that.
(And cool – you needn't wear a hat).

Like me, you may not like bamboo.
But there you will, I promise you!

Moving

To own a garden – nice to do,
but not when it starts owning you.
It's sad to leave a place behind
because the work's become a bind.

But then, a garden's far less pleasure
the day it takes up *all* your leisure.
My sister Sue has had to go,
with too much land and grass to mow.

It's tough not taking things with you
and settling for a lesser view.
Of course, you'll shed a load of tears.
You've loved your garden all those years.

But wait. The next one, though it's small
will soon have you within its thrall.
Sometimes it's quite fun downsizing.
You may find it quite surprising.

And if there's far less work to do,
your friends can see much more of you.
I know how much I'd hate to go.
I'd hate to leave my patch, I know.

I'm sometimes glad I've only got
a simple, undemanding plot.
But even then, it goes to pot
because I am away a lot.

As long as there's a bit of space
I'll wear a smile upon my face.
What's more, I'm sure you'll have one too,
if move you must. Good luck to you!

Broke

The kiss of the sun for pardon,
a lunch on the lawn for mirth –
one is closer to God in a garden
though planting one out costs the earth.

One is closer to broke in a garden
then anywhere else that I know,
and it frequently makes my heart harden
when things I have chosen don't grow.

I've planted a whole load of failures
and plants that just won't stay alive,
like sweet peas and climbers and dahlias,
where other things happily thrive.

There's nothing like planting a garden
for making one's soul so content,
but disasters do make my heart harden
when thinking how much I have spent!

Metre from 'God's Garden'
by Dorothy Frances Gurney (1858 – 1932).

Pelting down all week

Monday:
I will not plant today.
Outside it's rain and thunder.
Inside I'll have to stay.
I'm cross, and little wonder.

Tuesday:
Can't plant again today.
Two days of heavy raining.
I'll have to stay away.
No wonder I'm complaining.

Wednesday:
Another rainy day,
and no sign of it stopping.
And gardening? There's no way.
No wonder that I'm hopping.

Thursday:
My mood is worse today.
I'm feeling truly grizzly.
It's miserable and grey,
and yet again, it's drizzly.

Friday:
It's sheeting down again.
It truly is heartwrenching.
My garden's a flood plain.
Another bloody drenching.

Saturday and Sunday:
The rain won't go away.
This really isn't funny.
Please God, hear what I say
and make tomorrow sunny!

One thing I don't like about my garden

It's noisy – it's too near Heathrow,
where planes are flying pretty low,
and sixty planes in just two hours
is not much fun when tending flowers.
I cannot hear a blackbird sing
when all those planes are on the wing!

And now they're building right next door
and putting in a basement floor
we have the sound of drills as well,
so now the decibels are hell.
And that's not counting noisy trips
exchanging all the rubbish skips.

Though even in a country lane
the noise can be an awful pain
with motorways and rookeries
and microlites and bypasses
and saws and farm machinery.
Few hours will go past silently.

On top of that, there's hunting, shooting,
and all the noise from road re-routing.
And open days and festivals
are piling on the decibels.
Tranquillity is getting rare.
It's getting worse, the noise out there.

Gifts for gardeners

All garden centres nowadays
are crammed with things I'd never use,
although the very fact they're there
suggests that profits are good news.

Would I wear a garden apron?
No. Sensible, but not for me.
And mine (a gift) has not been used.
I don't think it will ever be.

A mini barrow, stacked with flowers.
Again, I'd find that somewhat twee.
A marvellous gift for somebody,
although that person isn't me.

And trendy urns? Once more I'd pass,
preferring softer terracotta,
and not much liking modern pots
however clever was the potter.

A seed box, 'SEED BOX' written on it –
another thing I'd find too twee.
I have one here, a Christmas gift
that's used for storing cutlery.

And flower place mats can be nice,
although I think I'd place a bet
gardeners have enough already
and wouldn't want another set.

No gardener wants to seem ungrateful –
we'd hate to see the giver miffed.
But maybe simple garden tokens
would make a rather better gift.

Leaf shapes

Palmate, Ovate, Serrate, Peltate,
Crenate, Oblong, Mucronate,
Elliptic, Dentate, Digitate,
Cuspidate, Attenuate.
Cuneate, Perfoliate,
Rhomboidal and Emarginate.
Acute and Cleft and Ciliate,
Oval, Obtuse, and Truncate.
Filiform, Trifoliate,
Obovate and Bipinnate.
My God, who ever learns all that?
Not me, I've left it far too late!

*I only know a few people who might recognise all our many leaf
shapes – like my botanist friends Hugh Synge and John Akeroyd,
who kindly checked this and my last book, weeding out any
botanical inaccuracies.*

*I think it's time I turned over a new leaf and started to learn a bit
more about the fascinating formations above!*

Monty Don

Just when I've switched to Monty Don,
the moment that his programme's on,
the phone goes. Leave it? No, I can't,
and then I miss a lovely plant.
Please don't call me when I'm viewing
Monty Don and what he's doing!

Oh, for greener fingers!

Oh, much, much greener fingers
some gardening friends have got.
I don't much like my fingers
as green they're often not.

I've seen much greener fingers
in someone else's place.
My fingers cannot match theirs,
but green can be my face!

I'm not that good at gardening,
but love it all the same.
My head is in the right place.
My fingers are to blame!

July

This is the weather that gardeners love,
and so do I.
Long summer hours, and beautiful flowers.
A big blue sky.
The beds and the borders are at their best;
it's time for a rest now the garden's dressed.
Now the work's all done, we are not hard-pressed.
Glad? So am I.

This is the weather that gardeners love,
and so do I.
Days to laze in the sun, the planting done,
the sun so high,
Time to take a pause and forget the chores
and look at the plants that we have outdoors
and feel proud of ourselves, and with just cause.
Our spirits fly!

Metre from 'Weathers'
by Thomas Hardy (1840-1928)
'This is the weather the cuckoo likes.
And so do I.'

Time to let things go a bit

Let the ramblers ramble,
let self-sowers sow.
Too much order – boring.
At times, let gardens go.

Don't go out there strimming.
Leave the place to grow.
Forget about the trimming –
at least a month or so.

Let it do its own thing.
You may well find your show
becomes a lot more pleasing
without your fork and hoe!

Four leafed clovers

If you find a four leafed clover,
look again – you may find many.
The chances are the clump's a freak
and four leafed ones are two a penny.

I've filled up eggcups with such clovers.
With luck I've certainly been blessed.
And if you find a four leafed clover,
do search again and find the rest!

I've not yet read a flower book
corroborating this is true.
But certainly it's worked for me.
The very best of luck to you!

The Marianne North Gallery
at Kew Gardens

Incredible! Quite fabulous!
Astonishing was Marianne.
Do see her gallery at Kew.
Do see her paintings if you can.

Flowers and plants in distant jungles
all painted in the blazing sun,
with dangerous snakes and insects there –
yet masterpieces, every one.

Thirty, forty years of painting
while dressed in stifling bombazine,
before the days of insect sprays
and with few means of keeping clean.

Years and years of endless toiling
in jungles painting plants and trees,
in temperatures of heat quite boiling –
sometimes thirty plus degrees.

Her very last bequest to us –
a splendid, gorgeous gallery
that stands within the grounds of Kew.
A truly lovely place to be.

Three hundred paintings, maybe more
await you once you're through the door.
Walk in; it's quite astonishing.
And what's more, there's an upper floor.

Do pay a visit if you can.
The Marianne North Gallery
is truly quite miraculous.
I'm sure you'll love it, just like me!

Plants and music

Do plants respond to music?
Some say it helps them grow.
It's said that they like opera.
I thought I'd like to know.

In France, I gave them Mozart,
and was it by sheer chance
they seemed to grow more quickly
and look more happy plants?

In England I tried rock bands –
the truly heavy stuff.
They wilted by that evening
and said they'd had enough.

I gave them country music
and lots of songs by Dolly.
Ms Parton made the garden
a lot more bright and jolly.

Do plants respond to music?
Well, now I think they do.
But take care what you play them,
or they'll complain to you!

(It's also said that music
can help our veg to grow,
which could explain the giants
that win the Best in Show!)

*Recommended: Mozart, Handel, Bach (not Rachmaninov),
Schubert, Dolly Parton, Johnny Cash, Benny Goodman, Maria
Callas.*
Not recommended: Garage, Funk, Hip-Hop, Acid Rock.

Why bees give me a buzz

It's funny when bees land on plants.
The weight of them brings down each stem,
but even so, the bees hold on.
It doesn't seem to worry them.

The plant stems lurch and quite a bit,
as much as thirty-five degrees,
but landing there and taking off
our bees achieve with graceful ease.

When flying in or flying off,
bees truly demonstrate their brains.
There never was a better jet –
they're perfect little aeroplanes!

Clever little helicopters,
taking off from just one spot,
even when the stem is wobbling.
I marvel at the bees I've got.

I'm sure you've never seen a bee
that topples, wobbles in mid-air
or crashes as a plane might do.
No jet or airbus can compare.

They fly with ease from flower to flower
and always with a perfect landing
on every bloom to which they zoom.
It quite defies my understanding.

Pubs

Hanging baskets, tubs and shrubs,
and flowerpots dotted here and there.
My goodness, pubs have woken up
to garden lovers everywhere!
It wasn't all that long ago
there wasn't any plant in sight.
The only pot? For cigarettes.
But these days they have got it right.
'The Jolly Gardeners' – names like that
are often on the signs of pubs.
And plenty of our hostelries
are looking more like garden clubs.

Publicans – congratulations!
It's nice to go and have a drink
where flowers are blooming everywhere
and landlords know how gardeners think.

Weedy?

Weeds are anything but weedy,
more tough than any cultivar.
How strange we ever call them 'weeds'
as that's the last thing that they are.
Weeds they're not, and never will be,
and weeds they never were, and aren't –
splendid fighters and survivors,
and keep them down, we often can't.
To say a person is 'a weed'
should be the greatest flattery.
How odd we choose to use this word
and do that so insultingly.

My first job

I landed my first job at seven.
And what was it I had to do?
Help out in a nursery garden
at weekends, for a hour or two.

I planted many trays with seeds.
My little finger – perfect tool!
I did that every Saturday
and on my holidays from school.

They paid me pennies for my time,
but I adored my Saturdays.
That nursery garden opposite
was what gave me the gardening craze.

Every weekend, planting seedlings –
for me that job was utter heaven.
Those little things can change one's life,
and planting there changed mine at seven.

'Perfect happiness, even in memory, is not common.'
– *Emma,* Jane Austen

True, I think, of most of us.
But in the case of gardeners, less.
Alone in dreams, alone outside,
one can feel perfect happiness.

Not common, I'll admit to that.
Not common, perfect happiness,
but commoner in gardeners –
that sense of great contentedness.

Loss of freedom

It makes one sound so old to say
that kids fared better in our day –
building camps and playing conkers
without the council going bonkers,
and going on a cycle ride
without a parent at our side.

Ah, what it was to go exploring
all by ourselves. With parents? Boring!
We climbed up trees and sat by seas
and looked for starfish unattended.
How sad it is those days have ended.

Of course life now is not the same.
Of course the parents aren't to blame.
Of course the world's a different place,
especially with less outside space.
So many now live in a city
without a garden – more's the pity.

A garden is that great first link
and with the wider world, I think.

It's where we started to explore
and right outside our own back door,
and grazed our knees, saw birds and trees –
all part of what a garden's for.

Back then, it was that outside space
that made the world a better place.
Without a garden, what a shame –
one reason life is not the same.

Singing to cows

Have you ever sung to cows?
I have – they seem to love a song.
I sit and sing upon the gate,
and lots of cows soon come along.

'Tom Dooley' seems to go down well.
You'll soon have quite a gathering.
It seems to be their favourite song –
that's not just my imagining.

A moo, I think, would be a boo.
But no, they listen silently.
It's quite amazing how a cow
can hear you out so patiently.

I know it's mad to sing to cows,
but love a song they clearly do.
You're at the gate, they're round the field,
but sing, and they will come to you.

A splendid audience they are –
they look at you with melting eyes.
My husband tells me I can't sing.
Cows disagree – a nice surprise!

Blindingly obvious

At times I do not use my eyes
as well as other gardeners do.
Our lawn had shrunk to half its size
without me seeing that was true.

For years it had been closing in
with shrubs extending on the lawn,
until it was a handkerchief
and looking tiny and forlorn.

How could I not have noticed that?
Perhaps I didn't want to see,
with all that work to chop shrubs back.
The task would take a month or three.

One pair of eyes is not enough.
I need four eyes, or six or eight
to tell me something's going wrong
until it's all too much, too late!

I'm glad to say the lawn is back
to what it was, its former size,
and things are nicely back on track –
but only thanks to other eyes!

Please keep your distance!

I don't much like it when I'm cooking
if people stand right over me.
I always feel that they are thinking
they would have done things differently.

It's much the same when I am gardening.
I don't like people standing there
and watching me as I am planting,
but ask myself, why do I care?

A feeling that they're somehow thinking
when they are standing feet away
(although I'm sure I'm being silly)
that they would not do things my way.

I wish they'd simply take a deckchair
and read a paper in the sun.
Do *you* hate people watching you?
I'm sure I'm not the only one.

If only they would keep their distance.
That's something that I'd never say,
although I can't bear hoverers
who watch me from one foot away!

Salt-filled pails

A salt-filled pail is where each snail
should truly meet its maker.
But then you'd need a hundred pails
for every quarter acre.

So many snails upon my plot!
Too many there for counting.
Oh, hundreds of them, such a lot.
I'm sure the number's mounting.

When wet, it's full of snails, my place.
And how I hate that crunching
when pottering my outside space
where snails are busy munching.

At night time, then it's even worse
when snails are busy dining.
I should put out a load more pails
and get on with the brining!

The plop, plop, plop as in they drop
would be most satisfying,
and not, I hope, a painful way
for snails to do their dying.

Beatrix Potter

Foxes,
rabbits,
cabbage patches,
ducks and hedgehogs,
dragonflies –
Potter shaped the way I see things,
she gave me a new pair of eyes.

Lilies,
squirrels,
owls and birds' eggs,
the world of natural history.
I owe a lot to Beatrix
from when her books were read to me.

Fir cones,
swallows,
tree bark, burrows –
in infancy she changed my eyes
and taught me how to look at things
with pleasure, wonder and surprise.

Children's writers,
children's artists –
they're sculptors of the way we see.
A bookless childhood?
That's so sad.
It's nothing short of tragedy.

My smashing husband

If you ever get the chance
to buy a place in southern France,
remember it can take all day
to dig the smallest patch of clay.

My husband dug a bed for me
to mark an anniversary.
A rose bed – gorgeous! Lovely present.
But digging it was most unpleasant.

And then, with tender, loving care
he planted several bushes there.
What nicer present could there be?
And all done so goodheartedly!

At last the border was complete,
and planted in the baking heat.
Of course I piled on endless praise –
the digging took him days and days.

But so exhausted then was he,
he ached all over miserably,
and rested up for two whole days,
while I prepared him meals on trays.

This story ends with quite a laugh
(though less so for my other half).
Our neighbour came round one day later –
'Voila, Liz!'
A rotovator!!

War zone

He's always gone for striking plants –
lots of statement, lots of colour,
while she prefers a subtle look.
He thinks that there's nothing duller.

He's keen on growing lettuces,
and she likes making lettuce soup.
And that makes him quite furious –
'Why waste them in this tasteless gloop?'

He's sneaked in yet another bush.
She thinks they have far too many,
and she's sad it's not a fuschia –
he will not allow her any!

'They're far too fussy for my taste.'
'For yours perhaps, but not for mine.'
She stomps off back into the house
to pour herself a glass of wine.

He likes the lawn all emerald green.
She likes to see odd daisies there.
He hates the mowing lines to show,
another thing she cannot share.

'I don't like lawns that look that smooth,
reminds me of a putting green.'
'Don't look at it.' 'How can I not?
Why *do* you have to be so mean?'

He likes a trellis, so does she.
On that the couple *do* agree.
But just what plant to grow round it
is causing further misery.

'He thinks that *he* has all the taste.'
'She thinks that *she* has all the flair.'
They'll say that if you visit them
each time the other one's not there.

Best to make just one the gardener,
as two of you can be a crowd,
especially with different tastes
on just what plants should be allowed.

The funny thing about this pair –
not one has been victorious,
but different tastes have worked a treat –
their garden is quite glorious!

However, gardening in a pair can work a treat

The proof of the pudding is Harold and Vita.
They were great partners, a fabulous team.
Proof you can garden well in a twosome,
and make the garden an absolute dream.

Just how well a collaboration can work is perhaps never more clear than it is at Sissinghurst in Sussex – the joint creation of Vita Sackville-West and her husband, Harold Nicholson. She did the planting while he planned the layout, and the result is a stunning example of successful teamwork.

Why do we do all the weeding?

Why do women do the weeding?
I've rarely met a chap who weeds
(except paid gardeners). So unfair,
as weeding's boring – all one needs!

Just like gardens, we're too weedy.
And far more women should complain
when we're left to do the weeding.
Why leave the job to us again?

Gardening hands

One knows another gardener by their hands.
They're always older than a gardener's face.
Real gardeners don't wear gloves, I often find.
They need to 'feel' if plants enjoy their space.

Our hands, too often scratched and spilling blood.
We should resort to wearing gloves again.
Smooth, pretty gardening hands – such rarities.
It's fortunate most gardeners aren't vain.

But gardeners' faces – often so content.
I notice that at every flower show.
Our gardens calm us, that is evident.
It's good for us to see a garden grow.

Absentminded

Rusty keys found in a flowerpot.
Wet spectacles left on the lawn
by the chair where I was reading –
and found when I went out at dawn.

A mug of tea left by the fuchsias.
A glass of wine, now full of ants.
A line of washing I'd forgotten –
a row of sodden bras and pants.

A hand fork, one not seen for ages,
and found half buried in the earth.
A mobile found inside a trug.
I hate to think what that was worth.

A newspaper, a horrid sight –
its pages hanging in a tree,
blown up there by the wind last night.
Can't get them down. Too high for me.

A watch I must have taken off
some years ago, and left to rust.
So absent-minded, that is me.
And get more organised, I must!

Fred West

As a freelance copywriter
you take on very different tasks,
until you're not surprised to hear
the sort of thing each client asks.

And one, a chain of garden centres,
needed several leaflets done
on patios and paving tips.
I thought the task might be quite fun.

They gave me lots of information,
but told me; 'If you find it hard,
here's a fellow who can help you',
and handed me a business card.

The name – Fred West – a local fellow.
'You may wish to give Fred a call,
or visit him up here in Gloucester,
that's if you're ever stuck at all.

He helps us out from time to time –
a freelance worker, just like you,
and good at things like paving stones.
I'd call him up, if I were you.'

Thank God, *thank God* I didn't call.
Would I be here? God only knows.
Of course, he knew just what to do
with paving stones and patios.

*Fred West (1941-1995) alone, and later with his second wife,
Rosemary, abused in a terrifying way numerous women and girls
(including family members), murdering at least 11 of them, some of
whom were found buried in the Wests' garden under patio and
paving stones.*

'Wind in the Willows'
by Kenneth Grahame

Grahame made me love all badgers.
He also made me love all moles.
However much they spoil a lawn,
I think of them as friendly souls.

And if you've ever read his book,
you may be into badgers too,
and cannot go along with culling
as many other people do.

I cannot help but picture Badger
with Mr Mole, and sipping tea.
Kenneth Grahame wrote about them
so beautifully and touchingly.

However fast that moles dig holes
depositing unsightly clumps,
I'm sure if you're a fan of Grahame
you'll think of them as friendly chumps.

Of course it worries me that badgers
may be threatening cattle farming,
but if you've ever read his book
you may find culling them alarming.

A thought for Interflora

Here's a thought for Interflora –
a competition with a prize
we flower fans would love to win.
I hope that you're all ears and eyes!

WIN A BOUQUET EVERY WEEK,
TO BE DELIVERED TO YOUR DOOR!
But tell us when you go away,
and say, of course, just how long for!

I hope you're reading, Interflora.
Now *that* I'd truly love to win.
I cannot always pick a bunch,
the state the garden's often in.

And not all partners are romantic.
I'm sure it's accurate, my hunch
that bouquets don't arrive that often.
How great to get a weekly bunch!

Roses are red

Roses are red, violets aren't blue.
Someone was mad, colour blind, too!

Roses are red. Some are, that's true.
Not all are red. Only to you.

Sugar is sweet – got that bit right.
Nothing wrong there, just with your sight.

Poets – all mad. Some are blind too.
Some needed specs. That much is true.

Tony Hannaford

Friend Tony is a marvellous painter.
Allotments are his greatest muse.
He paints his plot and quite a lot –
as if he has no time to lose.

Allotment scenes – quite beautiful.
Do you have an allotment too?
Perhaps you'd like to see his work,
and maybe he could paint for you.

Allotment wars

Oh dear! Poor Tony's been evicted!
Three cards – white, then red and yellow.
They told him he was too untidy.
I'm so, so sorry for the fellow.

'A huge committee – twenty people –
has told me to get off my plot.
They said I couldn't go on painting
and leave the place to go to pot.

They told me that I ought to know
the plot is not a studio,
and now, wherever can I go?
It's come as the most awful blow.'

P.S. I'm very glad to hear that Tony (anthonyhannaford.com) has now been re-instated, but only after being called to a pompous meeting attended by 20 people, and not without hours of petty arguing. Allotments, it seems, are becoming more and more like battlefields or board meetings!

Sorry, garden

The garden's crying out to me;
'Please, Liz, here's where you ought to be.
Please finish it, your wretched book,
and come outside and take a look!

I cannot wait another day
for you to put your book away.
Please finish it, and think of *me*!
And do that pretty speedily!

And Liz, what if it doesn't sell
and all your plants are then unwell?
Please Liz, do finish it and soon –
preferably this afternoon.

Another thing that's so unfair –
I bet you've got a drink in there.
I'm parched out here, *I* need a drink.
A wee bit selfish, don't you think?

Please come outside, and bring the hose.
Do water me, and right now please!
It's roasting, boiling hot out here.
It must be thirty three degrees!

The plants are sick and tired of you,
and now the grass is almost white,
and what are we supposed to do
while you keep writing day and night?'

Woodland Wonders

*'It's time for woodland walks,
it's time to catch a leaf,
and stare at stunning trees
in utter disbelief.'*

Older gardeners

Muddy wellies
green or black.
No trendy trugs –
a plastic sack.
No raffia,
just balls of string.
No decking,
no steel anything.
No whacky grasses,
no chic hat.
That's not where
older heads are at.

Younger gardeners

Trendy wellies,
always clean.
Border grasses –
white, not green.
Knot patch, perhaps.
No barbecue –
fire bowl instead.
More mirrors too.
More geometry,
things Japanese,
but garden aids
like kneelers?
Please!

Where have spring and summer gone?

Where have spring and summer gone?
Too soon passing.
Where have spring and summer gone,
some time ago?
Time – too quickly marching on.
Years go faster, every one.
Fading plants at every turn.
Now it's simply leaves to burn.

Where have all the warm days gone?
Too soon passing.
Where has all that sunshine gone,
some time ago?
Where have flowering shrubs all gone?
Into dormancy, each one.
Far less colour, with less sun.
Gardening is far less fun.

Where has time so quickly gone?
Too soon passing.
Where have lunches outside gone,
some time ago?
Where have all the clouds all gone?
Up in skies and every one.
Falling leaves at every turn.
Months ahead with more to burn.

With apologies to Pete Seeger and his poignant song;
'Where have all the flowers gone'.

Autumn leaves

Gorgeous when they're flying, wind-tossed,
autumn leaves are hard to beat,
but not when slushy, pock-marked, blackened
and slippery underneath our feet.

Fabulous in autumn woodlands,
when you have small kids with you.
Catching falling windswept leaves
is always a fun thing to do.

But, when blanketing our gardens,
those leaves are not a pleasant view –
simply tedious reminders
of all the work we'll have to do.

October

Pruning, over-wintering,
lifting, storing and transplanting,
digging corms before the frosts –
not a time I find enchanting.

Checking lawns for proper drainage,
tining, weeding, scarifying,
preparing ground for future turf.
The work out there is mind-defying.

Will I do what I'm supposed to?
Well, some tasks yes, but others no.
If the garden is a workhouse,
I'd sometimes rather let it go.

Remember, remember,
the fifth of November

Remember, remember
the fifth of November,
but don't have a fire on your plot,
as hedgehogs make digs
quite often in twigs.
For them, a great day it is not.

Remember, remember
this coming November,
for hedgehogs a great day it's not.
And some may expire
right there in the fire
as soon as it starts to get hot.

Remember, remember
this coming November
to check out the pile that you've got.
The poor little hogs
among all your logs
are right not to like you a lot.

Stick to the fireworks,
don't threaten hedgehogs,
please check out the pyre on your plot.
It's simply not fair
to animals there.
Here's hoping you *do* give a jot!

The fig

Adam chose the strangest tree
to hide his masculinity.
How could the fellow think of it?
The fig leaf is in five parts split!

Five slits in every single leaf –
his choice of leaf, beyond belief!
What's more, they're light, so when winds blew
his tackle must have been on view.

How *could* he pick a leaf of fig
to cover up his thingmagig?
A truly crazy leaf to choose
with other larger ones to use.

The fellow chose the strangest tree
and must have walked most cautiously,
or maybe he quite liked to see
Eve blush at his immodesty.

With rhubarb leaves, I would suggest
he would have been far better dressed.
They're larger, and without a gap –
much better clothing for the chap.

Solace

Bad day today, sad day today.
A great, great friend has passed away.
I need to be upon my own,
not answering the telephone.
I need to be among my flowers
and with their special soothing powers.
A garden – kind at times like this –
reflecting on a friend you'll miss.

The messages that gardens send
can help you cope with someone's end.
When sad news strikes, it's good to find
a garden space can be so kind.
At times like this, you need some space.
There's nothing like your outdoor place.

Built-in obsolescence

The broom handle's snapped. Most garden bags split.
Disposable world – I'm fed up with it.
The plastic pots chip. The trellis is bust.
Fork out on new stuff? I guess that I must.
The long arm has jammed; expensive one too.
Oh, so many things don't last the year through.
The mower's packed up, and now what to do?
A fortune to mend – I'll have to buy new.
Tools used to last ages, not any more,
so much less rugged than tools were before,
and makers all know it, that is for sure.
Now, when they're past it, it's quite clear to me,
death coincides with the time guarantee.

A lost childhood outside

Bows and arrows, somersaulting,
blood brothers, sisters – penknives out!
Building dams and minnow collecting,
and all with no grown-ups about.

Leapfrog races, jumping roofs,
bruises on our limbs and faces,
camps, tree houses, wobbly tents –
and often pitched in windy places.

River swimming, cliff top walking,
canoeing and three-legged races.
High jumps – no soft landing that.
Hazards in all outside spaces.

Standing on the top of weirs
while grasping on to willow trees.
No honour then in smooth young shins
without a plaster on our knees!

And building sites – all heaven-sent –
the loveliest of childhood places,
with tubs of wet cement to flip
at other children's hair and faces!

Roundabouts with asphalt round them
and not one rubber-matted swing.
Trolleys cobbled from old prams
with children collecting everything.

Cycle races down steep hills
without one gear and no free wheels.
Parents quite content with that
unless we turned up late for meals.

Walks alone in parks and woodlands
(of course, without a mobile phone),
and never scared of whom we'd meet
when out exploring on our own.

Empty buildings – fascinating!
We couldn't wait to see inside.
How we loved our independence.
What's more, it gave our parents pride.

Gosh, how dangerous was our childhood –
risks and hazards each time out.
I very often pause and wonder
exactly why I'm still about.

But then, at times I sometimes ask
if modern kids are too protected,
less able now to cope with things
now every danger *is* expected.

Ugh!

Ugh! Snails on window panes
revolt me when it rains.
That quite does in my brains.

I hate to see inside them.
Their innards – can't abide them.
I wish the snails would hide them.

It's horrible, the jelly
that's on the underbelly –
a beastly, frilly melée.

Snails on windows crawling,
or stuck there, glued and stalling –
a sight I find appalling!

Good tip for autumn

Cover your mint bed all over with straw,
then, when it's blanketed, set it alight.
Excellent killer of spores above ground,
and good for all rhizomes suffering blight.

Out roasting chestnuts

I remember, out in our drive,
while our old neighbours were still alive,
roasting chestnuts in the nip of November.
I'll always remember.

Two dear souls.
I tended the coals,
while in the cold chill of that Autumn evening
they smiled as if in heaven,
merry on sherry.
The chestnuts were done.
It was all such fun.

And then a policeman turned up from our local station,
and mentioned a complaint about the smoke.
He shook his head.
'I'm sorry.'
Nice bloke.
'We had a call from the woman next door.'
(A loner, a moaner, a constant bore).

'I won't report this' said the nice young man.
'And eat those chestnuts if you can!'

'Would you like one?' I asked.
'Why not?' he said.
'And then please put that barbecue to bed,
although there's far less smoke then your neighbour said.'

The old girls. Gone. And how I miss them here,
especially when November nights are near.
I think of them, and that pleasant policeman
standing here in our drive
when the neighbours were still alive
and cheerily chomping chestnuts.

Ouch!

I'm leaning down to pull a weed
and slip a disc – that's *all* I need!
The weed's still happy in that bed,
and now I'm stuck in mine instead.

Too late I learned the simple trick
of capping every bamboo stick.
It should have come as no surprise
the sticks have stabbed me in both eyes.

The steps are slippery, down I fall,
and cannot grab on to the wall.
My knee is hurting quite a bit,
I wonder if I've broken it.

It's pelting and a sudden slip
now tells me I've done in my hip.
I haven't got my mobile phone,
and now I'm out here all alone.

Oh, just how dangerous gardening is.
It's full of dire calamities.
A hundred hazards wait out there.
I truly must take greater care!

In autumn years

In autumn years one's memory
is not quite what it used to be,
and names escape one frequently.

And not just people's names, that's true
(though that is bad enough to do)
but plant names too, and quite a few.

Whatever can that flower be?
Whatever is it called, that tree?
Some names just won't come back to me.

And then I can't consult a book.
No book will get me off the hook
because I won't know where to look.

Without its name, the glossary
will now be of no help to me.
Frustrating – fading memory.

I'll have to plough through every page
and that, of course, will take an age.
I guess most gardeners reach this stage!

N<small>OW</small> I<small>S THE</small>
S<small>EASON OF</small> M<small>Y</small> D<small>ISCONTENT</small>

'Now is the winter of my discontent
as far too fast the former seasons went.

And now I rarely go outside first thing,
too cold to be outside and wandering.

These days, I don't rise early from my bed.
Less fun with plants in dormancy, or dead.'

January

This is the weather that gardeners hate,
and so do I.
It's so bloody grey and it rains each day;
it makes me sigh.
Now it's nothing but clearing leaves away
and it's only the jobs that bring dismay,
and with skies above that are wet and grey,
and little out there that's bright and gay
and it's pelting again like yesterday.
Cross? So am I.

This is the weather that gardeners hate.
And so do I.
In winter my whinges multiply
as days go by.
Now there's nothing to grow, and few blooms blow.
Oh, and most of my show died months ago,
and there's nothing to do but rake and hoe
or slip on the ice and shovel the snow,
and it's freezing out there, it's ten below.
Cross? So am I!

Wintering plants in France

For years all our geraniums
were, over Winter, sadly lost.
We did our best protecting them,
but they succumbed to snow and frost.

A heated greenhouse? So expensive,
especially if you're months away.
Burning money – never funny –
with heating left on every day.

And, with shutters at the windows,
we never thought they'd stay alive.
No light, no water, all those months.
However could our plants survive?

They did! On every single stalk
we noticed tiny specks of green.
It seems that they can stay alive
however dark and cold it's been.

We pruned them back to inches high –
'our babies' – a nice name for them,
and they survived to our surprise –
yes, every last geranium.

It seems they do not need a drink
or else to see the light of day,
or have some type of heating there.
A nice surprise, I have to say.

We couldn't quite believe our eyes,
and many thanks to our friend, Hugh,
for giving us such great advice
and telling us just what to do!

December

Like many people, I like Winter Jasmine
and other plants that do not mind the cold,
and trees with pretty fruits like Callicarpa –
they cheer me when the year is getting old.
And Wintersweet's a plant that's hard to beat –
a gorgeous yellow, like our Aconites.
Winter has her share of nice surprises.
Our gardens are not stripped of all delights.

But then, I do not like the nip,
and if it's freezing, fear I'll slip,
and black spot I don't like a lot,
what's more, it's always on my plot.
You love the winter? I do not –
not when the garden's gone to pot.

I've always much preferred my outside room
with jobs that do not give me any gloom,
and put off many tasks that should be done
because they're far less fun without the sun.

A Jenny Wren

When plants have died, and skies aren't blue
and days are grey with far less light
and outside there's so much to do
but not one job that brings delight,
a Jenny Wren upon a tree
then does her best to comfort me.

When gardeners rake until each eve,
and do not hear the time of clocks,
where mud's to tread and plants are dead
and tiredness makes us feel like crocks,
a Jenny Wren upon a tree
can sing so sympathetically.

When very little grows at all
and when our spirits start to fall
and gardening pleasures start to pall
with bags and bags of leaves to haul,
a Jenny Wren upon a tree
can lift one's spirits magically.

When all around us cold winds blow
and cheeks are red, and lips are raw,
when plants have died some months ago
and when the garden is a bore,
a Jenny Wren upon a tree
can be such soothing company.

Annuals and perennials

Annuals remind us of seasons,
but also remind us of death.
Annuals remind us of passing,
the day we will take our last breath.

Perennials, often more pleasing,
plants that are with us to stay.
Year after year reappearing,
plants that do not pass away.

Death in a garden is common.
Death in the winter is rife.
Perennials keep us more cheerful,
springing right back into life.

Honesty (Lunaria)

Beautiful when blossoming,
also lovely when it's dead.
Rub the seed pods in your fingers,
and now arrange dried flowers instead.
Beautiful, in snowy white –
it goes with any colour scheme
and always seems to catch the light.
In winter, honesty's a dream.
Outside, inside, years of pleasure,
a gorgeous purple in the spring,
then winter white, a pure delight,
a plant that goes with everything.

Lichens

Dank and drippy winter woodlands –
a winter walk is not much fun.
But still my husband drags me off –
and when there isn't any sun.

And why? Because he wants the lichens
that we can see on every tree.
The sight of all those fluffy plants
puts him in total ecstasy!

A model railway nut is he.
His railway – couldn't live without it.
And lichens do make splendid trees.
They're great for that, no doubt about it.

At times I help him collecting lichens
to fill another plastic sack.
But *rocks*? No, there I draw the line
and leave him there, and trudge off back.

I'll pick him twigs to make his trees,
I'm really rather good at that.
But lifting rocks? What misery!
That's not quite where my head is at.

A winter walk is not much fun
when lugging rocks. That's not for me,
although they do look very good
among his mountain scenery!

Adonis

Adonis was the Grecian god
renowned for his attractive face,
but what is far less known of him
is that he loved all outside space.

He hated winter, did Adonis,
when nothing blossomed, nothing grew,
and flew off to the underworld
exactly as I'd like to do.

And there, within the underworld,
he waited patiently for spring.
He couldn't stand the wintertime
without a single budding thing.

Adonis was a wise young man.
I'd like to do the same as him.
Most gardeners like to get away
when outside it is wet and grim.

A clever fellow was Adonis –
he taught us all to get away
until the springtime brings the sun,
and have a winter holiday.

He flew off to the underworld,
I'd also like to fly down under
and get a bit of Ozzie sun
just like Adonis – little wonder!

When plants are dying

When plants are dying, do they know it?
Can a cut flower feel regret?
Can leaves be frightened when they're falling?
I'm pretty sure they can't,
and yet...

Do shrubs feel pain when gardeners prune them?
Do trees and branches fear the saw?
Are plants in any way like us?
We think they're not, but can't be sure.

Too big a challenge

A garden that thrills me
is not one that kills me
and doesn't allow me a break.
I wouldn't like owning
a very large garden
because of the time it would take.
But how I admire those
who do have large gardens,
and work there for hours every day.
I do like my leisure
and find it no pleasure
if I just can't be away.

Christmas trees

My God, that endless needle drop!
It never ever seems to stop.
And fairy lights upon the tree
will dry it out more rapidly.
Damn! Needles, needles everywhere,
all up the stairs and in my hair,
and even in our shoes and bed.
But buy a plastic tree instead?
Oh, no. I'd hate a plastic tree.
Now, that would *truly* needle me!

The greatest present is one you can't wrap

The greatest present for a child
is one they'd never ask you for:
a patch of earth to call their own,
and right outside your own back door.

Somewhere they can put some seeds in.
Somewhere they can call their own.
Somewhere they can call 'my garden'
and watch the way that something's grown.

Give a child a love of gardening –
so rarely given any more,
but sometimes, sometimes, when it is –
a gift they'll *truly* thank you for.

December and January

Indoor plants like hyacinths
are dotted around to bring me cheer,
as are daffs, although they're forced.
At Christmas time they're always here.
I know there's little out there now;
my garden has been put to bed.
But still I get my fill of plants;
they're all around the house instead.

I never understand a house
without a vase of blooms on view.
I'm sure you always have some flowers,
I'm pretty sure most gardeners do.
Without a daily dose of them,
it feels as it there's something wrong.
And with no soothing blossoms there,
we somehow feel we don't belong.

An ever faster world

The faster it becomes, this place,
the more we need an outside space.
The more we speed, the more we need
a break from the increasing pace.

The more we do, the more we rush,
the more we need a bit of hush
to take a break from everything.
There's nothing quite like gardening.